GREAT ROYAL DISASTERS

GREAT ROYAL DISASTERS

Lesley Cunliffe

With cartoons by Martin Honeysett

Arthur Barker Limited · London

A subsidiary of Weidenfeld (Publishers) Limited

Published in Great Britain by
Arthur Barker Limited
91 Clapham High Street
London SW4 7TA

ISBN 0 213 16938 X

Printed in Great Britain by
Butler & Tanner Ltd
Frome and London

Contents

Introduction   7

 1 Andrew   9
 2 Royal Art   11
 3 Royal Sex   29
 4 Embarrassing Relations   36
 5 Royal Food   38
 6 Royal Drama   48
 7 Royal Fashion   53
 8 Money   60
 9 Good Sport   62
10 Job Satisfaction   66
11 Royal Farts   70
12 Religion   72
13 Democracy   75
14 Royal Ceremonial   83
15 Drink   91
16 Royal and Rude   95
17 Foreign Affairs   103
18 Edward VIII   108
19 Endurance   112
20 Royal Children   116
21 Royal Deaths   119

5

Introduction

Most of us are not royal. This oftens comes as a shock to little girls who then take up riding with a vengeance. The Queen may be the only little girl to whom it came as a shock that she *was* a princess – when she already knew that she was keener on horses.

This slender volume is intended for closet fantasists whose parents may have been too poor to pay for riding lessons and for those who haven't yet discovered the relaxing hobby of genealogy – that is, for people who secretly envy the royal family. For it requires only the most superficial look into the royal cupboards (and archives and newspaper clippings) to discover how hideously embarrassing it can be to be royal. After reading this book, unroyal people will feel vastly content with their lot.

To be royal is unnatural by definition, and inconvenient. The whole business is fraught with misunderstanding – not least by royalty itself. If any of them had the sense to emulate the Emperors of Japan, who realised that the monarch is a mundane deity invented to meet a strong human need, this book would have been impossible to compile. But most of the recent British royal family (with the exception of our own dear Queen), infected by the eighteenth-century rationalism that Victoria's intellectually pretentious Prince Consort brought in his luggage from Germany, have made mistaken attempts at democracy.

Clumsy royal attempts at common-ness are most unwise. This is because royalty are untrained in ordinariness, and must learn it in public – an embarrassing business, and the basis of the most squirm-making Royal Disasters.

Interestingly enough, it was the Duchess of Windsor, born an American, who showed the most profound understanding of monarchy. She (who once said: 'I would like to be the head of an advertising agency') astutely observed of King Edward VIII: 'He was born to be a salesman. He would have made an admirable representative for Rolls-Royce. But a king cannot start selling motor-cars.'

The splendid woman saved us from such a king.

1 *Andrew*

Prince Andrew is so unbelievably boring and Sarah Ferguson is so unbelievably boring, that although they have intended to marry since childhood, it was clear that something would have to be done to make them acceptable to the British public, who have become accustomed to a rich diet of excitement since the rise in influence of the cheaper newspapers.

Prince Philip showed his characteristic executive streak by calling in a team of experts. During regular consultations with the Palace, a well-known market research firm invented the concept of the 'Royal Sloane Ranger'. An extensive media hype was climaxed by the hurriedly-assembled Lady Diana Spencer. She was a hit with the public, who elected her Princess of Wales.

This prototype revealed a few flaws, but there was sufficient time before the next royal wedding to deal with them. The worst snag – that there are no acceptable-looking young women in the upper classes without 'A Past' who have reached the age of consent – is at the bottom of the most brilliant PR coup of this century. Some have likened it to the invasion of Pearl Harbor.

The marketing men simply teamed up the problem – one sexually-obsessed second son of the monarch – with their large list of untalented sexually-cooperative young women possessed of a taste for celebrity and no scruples about accepting large cheques from the gutter press.

The show was on. One not-quite-actress after another titillated the public with accounts of their nights of love with 'Randy Andy', until exactly the right pitch was reached. When it was thought that the public could stand no more, the Palace wheeled on 'Miss Sarah Ferguson'. The hard planning, ingenious strategy, relentless efforts of this public-spirited team of marketing men paid off. The editor of a new high technology tabloid was beside himself: the latest royal bride, naturally a large smudge of Technicolor, was seemingly born for his paper, which until then had been in danger of failing. More to the point, as far as the Palace was concerned, Prince Andrew had acquired a dashing image, quite in keeping with the style of the young woman that the nation's Mrs Grundys were now eager to welcome. The Palace, with the aid of this now-famous PR firm, thus wrenched the conventional attributes for a royal bride into the twentieth century!

Prince Edward has already found the girl of his dreams. Her parents have filed for the now-obligatory divorce, and her mother has set up in Dallas with a Libyan trans-sexual, who often visits Princess Michael of Kent disguised as a chiropodist. The bride-to-be, sixteen, is herself in Gstaad being taught to sniff cocaine by a retired bi-sexual racing driver who is old enough to be her father. She has promised to return to England to take up a job in Sotheby's Erotic Art department as soon as she has got to page 180 of the Kama Sutra. Prince Edward, however, has not been keeping his part of the bargain, and the wedding, scheduled for 1990, may not take place as planned if he doesn't do something quickly about endearing himself to the 'gay community'. A recommendation which, to the extreme irritation of the marketing boys, he has so far seemed reluctant to take up. It is understood that he has inherited his mother's phobia of public lavatories.

2 *Royal Art*

When Patrick Lichfield developed his prints of the royal family group photograph in 1972, he realised that the special wide-angle lens he had used to get them all into the picture had distorted the extent of Princess Margaret's bosom, making it even more generous than it actually is. He apologised to the Princess, but as she considers her mammary attributes are among her best features, she was apparently happy to have them exaggerated.

For his official engagement photograph of the Prince and Princess of Wales, Lord Snowdon had the reasonably bright idea of re-creating Sir Joshua Reynolds's famous portrait of the Princess's ancestor, the beautiful Duchess of Devonshire, born Georgiana Spencer. As the Princess was still in possession of her puppy fat, and the only jewellery she possessed aside from the gold 'D' she wore around her neck was her £28,000 engagement ring (a sapphire bought from a jeweller's catalogue, which drew attention to her badly-nibbled fingernails), it was decided to accept the loan of a distractingly impressive diamond necklace and some spectacular diamond chandelier ear-rings from Collingwood's, the jewellers, to add a touch of glamour to the portrait.

But the borrowed jewels turned out not to have been a good idea. After they were returned to Collingwood's, they were offered for sale in Amsterdam, accompanied by Snowdon's official photograph, and tagged with the sad story that the Spencers were selling the family jewels to pay for their daughter's wedding.

Despite the fact that he had flirted with communism and been friends with W.H. Auden and Stephen Spender, C. Day Lewis was appointed Poet Laureate following the death of John Masefield (who was, incidentally, such a modest man that he always sent his royal odes to *The Times* with a stamped addressed envelope, in case they should fail to please). C. Day Lewis took over in 1968, and flaunted tradition by choosing to publish his odes in the *Guardian* instead of *The Times*.

Both times the Poet Laureate met the Queen, something went wrong. At their first encounter he was mistakenly presented with a splendid plush-covered box containing the gold chain and badge of the Chancellor of the Order of St Michael and St John intended for Lord de l'Isle and Dudley, as the band discreetly played the theme from *Butch Cassidy and the Sundance Kid* – a favourite at investitures.

The last time he met his sovereign was a more informal occasion. He put his feet on what he assumed was a convenient footstool, but which turned out to be one of the corgis.

12

The old Duke of Gloucester, having sat through *Tosca* at Covent Garden on somebody's state visit, watched bored the whole way through until Maria Callas plunged over the battlements. Then his distinctive high-pitched voice rang through the opera house: 'Well, if she's really dead, we can all go home.'

The Times, reporting on a recently painted portrait of Queen Victoria, solemnly wrote: 'The Queen's bosom has been deliciously handled and has been brought out by the artist in full rotundity.'

One of the most doubtful compliments to the Queen was a poem written by Mrs Mary Wilson, wife of the former

Prime Minister, to commemorate her Jubilee. It goes:

> They love her for her wisdom and her pride
> Her friendship and quiet majesty.
> And soon the streets of Britain will be thronged
> With crowds rejoicing in her Jubilee.

C. Day Lewis's effort for the Prince of Wales's investiture suggested that the poet laureate had been moonlighting at a greetings card factory. He wrote:

> You, sir, inherit
> A weight of history in a changing world,
> Its treasured wisdom and its true
> Aspirings the best birthday gift for you.

Neither of these is a match for the style of the Scottish poet William McGonagall. He forthrightly celebrated Queen Victoria's Jubilee with the lines:

> And this is her first Jubilee Year
> And will be her last, I rather fear.

By the time of the coronation of King Edward VII, the Scottish bard's powers had begun to fail him, or more likely he just got bored with the subject, finding as others do, middle-aged Danish women exceedingly boring, for he wrote of Queen Alexandra in his Coronation Ode:

> The Queen, from first to last, was the crowning glory of
>   the ceremony,
> Her beauty, her grace, her exquisite dress was lovely to
>   see,

14

And her train of crimson and gold was borne by eight
  gentlemen
Which certainly was a great honour conferred upon them.

When John Buchan was presented to King George v in
1935, the King said to him: 'I don't get much time for
reading, but when I do I enjoy your books, *The 39 Steps*
and so on. Now, before you go, the Queen would like a
word with you.'

Buchan then had a word with Queen Mary, who said:
'The King does not get much time for reading and when
he does I am afraid that he reads the most awful rubbish!'

Prince Philip once referred to a Henry Moore sculpture
as 'a monkey's gallstone'.

Queen Victoria so admired *Alice in Wonderland* when it was first published that she wrote to Lewis Carroll sending her compliments, and adding that she would be greatly pleased to receive any other book of his. The flattered author sent her a copy of his *Syllabus of Plane Algebraical Geometry*.

His second effort to parry the Queen's irrepressible flirtatiousness was less subtle. She asked if she could have a photograph of the author. He refused to send her one. He explained to a young friend that he had replied: 'I was obliged to answer: "Mr Dodgson presents his compliments to Her Majesty, and regrets to say that his rule is never to give his photograph except to *young* ladies." I am told that she was annoyed about it, and said "I'm not so old as *that* comes to!"'

Carroll never liked even to acknowledge women past the age of puberty.

Queen Mary amassed an enormous collection of jade figurines, china, family portraits, miniatures, and anything else that took her fancy. Her collection was famous not

'A note from the Queen, thanking you for your
hospitality and generosity.'

simply for its extent but for the methods she used, for which some say extortion would not be too strong a word. The Queen's visits to large houses were often preceded by a judicious tucking-away of objects which were likely to appeal to her.

Often arriving uninvited, the Queen would stand in front of a covetable object and, while her host held his breath, would pronounce in measured tones: 'I am caressing it with my eyes.' If this hint was insufficient, the Queen would let the matter drop. But on taking her leave, would pause and with a look of touching entreaty ask: 'May I go back and say goodbye to that dear little cabinet?' If *that* failed to result in another acquisition, her letter of thanks might contain an offer to buy the piece. Few resisted the final assault.

One aristocrat, however, was quite capable of defending himself against Queen Mary's predatory activities. He possessed a piece of furniture about which the Queen felt such urgency that she could not be bothered to go through her usual coy routine. She came right out with it:

'I am going to do a dreadful thing. I have never seen anything I like so much as that chest and I am going to ask you to let me have it!'

This flirtatious approach fell on stony ground. Her host replied with great presence of mind: 'I am so sorry – but I could not possibly ask you to accept that chest because it is a *fake*!'

One of her ladies-in-waiting loyally defended the Queen's near-kleptomania, explaining: 'It is not greed – merely her desire to save anything worthwhile for the nation.'

'I do wish you musicians would not play *God Save The King* so quickly,' George V said testily to the conductor Sir Thomas Beecham after a concert at the Albert Hall. 'You hurry as if you wanted to get it over. You see, it means a great deal to me. I look upon it almost as a hymn.'

The Queen got the point of it from the start. When she was a very little princess, she replied *God Save The King* when her grandfather asked the name of her favourite song. She must have heard about the time when King William IV asked the infant Queen Victoria the same question, and got the same answer.

The Queen Mother, on the contrary, when watching television with friends, as the national anthem was played ordered them to pull the plug. 'Switch it off! Unless one's there it is embarrassing – rather like hearing the Lord's Prayer while playing canasta.'

The Duke of Windsor, who used to play *The Red Flag* on the banjo when he was at university, was unmoved by the national anthem until he arrived in England for his first visit after the Abdication and was only treated to one verse, which caused him to sulk.

Many consider the royal sense of humour a disaster area. Prince Charles in particular has been known to offend with what he seems to believe are successful puns. 'That just sleighed me!' (after going sledging with some Eskimos), and 'I bet they're having a whale of a time' (passing a whaling ship, on the same visit to Canada). He was thought to have been particularly pleased with 'I am

'It's just as well they're not playing "The Stripper".'

not accustomed in any way to unveiling busts . . . but now I shall complete the process of allowing my father to expose himself.' He came up with this one when he unveiled a bust of Prince Philip.

During her state visit to the USA in 1984 the Queen was given a grand banquet at the White House, with which Mrs Nancy Reagan intended to impress not only the Queen but the entire world. It was planned to the last detail, with the unfortunate exception of adequate intelligence about the eccentric sense of humour of the Marine Band. When the Queen and President Reagan took the floor to open the dancing, the band struck up a vigorous rendition of *The Lady is a Tramp*.

Alfred Austin was appointed Poet Laureate by Queen Victoria but survived into the reign of King George v, her grandson. He wrote such terrible stuff that even the Prime Minister asked why he was allowed to stay on. 'Because he wanted it,' replied the King, who was himself mostly interested in a quiet life.

Alfred Austin's most memorable lines were written on the illness of the Prince of Wales, later to reign as King Edward VII:

> Across the wires the electric message came:
> He is no better, he is just the same.

Augustus John was commissioned to paint a portrait of the Queen Mother, but he failed to turn up for the first sitting. The waiting Queen Mother was eventually delivered a telegram from the artist apologising for his absence, and saying that he was 'suffering from the influence'. He kept his subsequent appointments with enthusiasm, sustained by numerous bottles of brandy placed, at his sitter's hospitable suggestion, in a cupboard adjoining his easel.

When Robert Graves went to Buckingham Palace to receive the Queen's Medal for Poetry, he said to the Queen:

'How much longer are these portraits going to take?'

'I don't know if you realise, Ma'am, but you and I are both descended from the prophet Mohammed.'

'Oh, really,' replied the Queen.

'Yes.'

'How interesting.'

'I think', continued the poet, 'that you should mention it in your Christmas message because a lot of your subjects are Mohammedan.'

Sir Gerald Kelly was recommended by Kenneth Clark to paint portraits of the King and the Queen Mother just before the war broke out. While he was down at Windsor to put in a few finishing touches, war was declared. He remained at the castle, off and on, for the next five years. It was said that he would steal down to his studio in the dead of night to erase the previous day's work in order to prolong his stay.

Horrified by the vulgarity of a proposed extension to the National Gallery, which he likened to a carbuncle, the Prince of Wales delivered a polemic to the nation's top architects on the importance of good design.

Shortly afterwards it was pointed out that his own idea of taste was amply demonstrated by the *objets d'art* which had decorated his private apartments in Buckingham Palace. Most conspicuous was the herd of grotesque plush 'trolls', ranged along the mantelpiece. The two miniature chastity belts he employed to dispense lavatory paper and his probably unrivalled collection of 100 loo seats were thought to be equally telling.

Since the advent of the Princess of Wales the emphasis has been on the Laura Ashley style.

1936 was a bumper year for amateur international diplomacy. The actress Marlene Dietrich became convinced that if only she could meet King Edward VIII, she would most certainly be able to talk him out of his plan to marry Mrs Simpson. She telephoned his home persistently and asked to speak to him. When all her requests were refused, she hit upon the scheme of presenting herself one weekend at Fort Belvedere where the King spent his weekends. On being denied admission, she abandoned her scheme.

'I told him he could keep his collection, but only in its proper place.'

At a civic reception in Lusaka, the Queen was subjected to a long harangue in the form of a speech of welcome by the mayor, Mr Simon Mweme. In his ermine-trimmed robes and wearing a chain of office, the mayor ranted on about the War of Liberation and paused from time to time to invite the Queen to reply to his charges. 'No, thank you very much,' she responded patiently. This welcome was followed by some 'traditional spontaneous dancing' which turned out to be less than light-heartedly choreographed. The dancers were wearing white 'settlers shorts', bush jackets and pith helmets, and brandishing swagger sticks.

The mayor, colloquially known as 'Baby Elephant', claimed later: 'I did not offend the Queen.' When she left, the crowds chanted 'Bye Bye Queenie.'

Apparently her best moment of the trip was overhearing one African chief tell another a moment after meeting her 'My God, the Queen is a woman!'

Of the Queen's cousin, Lord Harewood, who has devoted most of his energies to the study and administration of opera, particularly at Covent Garden, the Duke of

Windsor once said: 'It's very odd about George and music. You know, his parents were quite normal.'

A royal pioneer in the divorce courts in order to legitimise his son by the Australian violinist Patricia Tuckwell, he paved the way for Princess Margaret when her time came.

Lord Harewood's first wife, Marion Stein, who was not a lucky woman, later married Jeremy Thorpe.

3 *Royal Sex*

Three teenaged girls who were sharing a room at a Scottish houseparty in 1975 were surprised to be woken by Prince Andrew, a fellow houseguest.

'There's a ghost in my room,' he said. The girls stared at him incredulously. 'There's a ghost in my room,' he repeated, 'and so I'll have to stay in this room with you.'

Managing to control their terror, the girls firmly rejected this proposal and he was returned to his own room.

On a tour to Zambia, the Queen's security men were delighted when they asked the names of their chauffeurs, two big burly black fellows. One said that he was called 'Adolf' and the other muscle-bound driver answered to 'Phyllis'.

During the Abdication crisis things were so chaotic that even the nursery was aware that something was amiss. 'What's happening?' little Princess Margaret asked her elder sister, the 10-year-old (unsuspecting) heiress presumptive. Lilibet replied with surprising imagination, 'I don't know really, but I believe Uncle David wishes to get married. I *think* he wants to marry Mrs Baldwin and Mr Baldwin doesn't like it!'

The Duke of Clarence, eldest son and heir of King Edward VII is widely thought to have been Jack the Ripper. Whatever the truth of this there is no doubt that he had a taste for adventure. *Punch* published a cartoon during his days as a Cambridge undergraduate. Eddy (for that is the name he was known by) is shown on a balcony of Trinity College, with two undergraduates looking up at him. 'Isn't it beautiful?' says one to the other, who replies: 'Too beautiful to look at.' The homosexual inference was obvious, and the heir to the throne was removed from the university forthwith.

Unfortunately, London abounded with even more exotic temptations, and it was not long before the prince began to frequent a notorious homosexual brothel off Tottenham Court Road. The Hundred Guineas Club which enjoyed a degree of fashion, required members to use women's names. It was considered extremely witty of him to employ the codename 'Victoria' in honour of his grandmother.

The irrepressible prince was soon sent on a trip to India, which in those days was regarded in the same light as Australia is today, as far as the royal family is concerned. There he had an affair with a laundryman in Shuttadore, which was immortalised in some extremely impure doggerel.

It is hard to understand how the solution to the perpetual embarrassment he caused to the royal family could be found in marriage to the young Princess May of Teck, whose abiding interest at the time was the study of algebra. But his death from a fever shortly before the wedding left her free to marry his younger brother, the future George V, who was also interested in science, as shown by his insistence upon having a barometer in every room.

The Duke of Windsor, who seems to have got into trouble whenever he took his clothes off, once emerged from bathing in the sea at Le Touquet with the appearance of a Red Indian, when the dye had come out of his bathing costume. On a later holiday, the notorious 'Nahlin' cruise, upon which he was accompanied by his inamorata, the multiply-married Mrs Simpson, the diminutive uncrowned King appeared on the front pages of the world's newspapers attired in nothing but the briefest pair of shorts. The public was scandalised as much by his tiny physique as by his relative nakedness, but it prepared some of them, at least, for a subsequent manifestation in his birthday suit in a Viennese bath house on the way home overland to England.

Princess Michael of Kent, who once told Jean Rook, the popular columnist, 'I have big shoulders and tiny boobs', horrified the royal family by issuing an official photograph to commemorate her fortieth birthday in which her hair, wantonly unloosed, flowed out over her naked shoulders. Whatever garment covered her nakedness was definitely off-camera.

Although she had for some time been aware of his existence, the Queen had never met her sister's friend Roddy Llewellyn. She was instantly shown what Princess Margaret saw in him when they bumped into each other in the nursery at Royal Lodge, where the male ingenu and Princess Margaret were weekending with the Queen Mother.

Informally clad in nothing but a pair of 'Y-fronts' and clutching a shirt and the button he hoped nanny would sew on it for him, Mr Llewellyn stammered out in confusion, 'Please forgive me, Ma'am, I look awful,' to which the Queen graciously replied: 'Don't worry, I don't look so good myself.'

Princess Margaret continued to be fond of the accident-prone young man after he announced his intention to marry someone his own age. 'I couldn't have afforded him much longer,' she said.

King William IV, who reigned for four years before Queen Victoria came to the throne, was so dull that he is only ever remembered in monarchical mnemonics. His young relative Victoria knew him as 'Uncle Pineapple' – affectionately referring to his distinctly pointed head. He proposed marriage and was refused by: Miss Catherine Tilney-Long; the Dowager Lady Elphinstone; the Dowager Lady Downshire; Miss Margaret Mercer Elphinstone; Lady Berkeley; the youngest daughter of the King of Denmark (madness in the family); the daughter of the Elector of Hesse-Cassel; and the Duchess of Oldenbourg (who found him 'definitely unpleasant').

He was eventually lucky in love and with patient resignation settled happily into marriage with Princess Adelaide of Saxe-Meiningen.

During a visit to the United States of America in 1971, Prince Charles was surprised to find himself in the constant company of Miss Tricia Nixon, the President's irritating elder daughter. President Nixon's dynastic ambitions became clear to the Prince of Wales when he left the two of them alone together in a room, saying, 'My wife and I will keep out of the way so that you can really feel at home.' Prince Charles was so horrified by the experience that he uncharacteristically reported upon his return that he found Miss Nixon 'artificial and plastic'.

The second President of the United States, John Adams, could be forgiven for *his* dynastic scheme on the grounds that he had not quite got the hang of democracy. In any event, he determined to marry his son to one of the many daughters of King George III. When George Washington heard about this, he went to Adams in a white uniform to try to talk him out of it. After failing, Washington returned for a further attempt, this time dressed in black. When even this failed, he arrayed himself in his Revolutionary War uniform and offered to run the President through with his sword.

Queen Victoria (who once had a portrait of her daughter Alice painted as a nun, her hands clasped in the presence of a vision of the recently departed Prince Albert) was discovered during the first months after his death immersed in a lurid book entitled *Confessions of a Priest*. She did not exhibit symptoms of Victorianism until late in life. When told that her childbearing days were over, she exclaimed, 'Oh, doctor, can I have no more fun in bed?' Fun was clearly not one of the Prince Consort's priorities, since all their married life he slept 'in a little sleeping suit with feet, like babies wear', as the Queen noted in her diary.

Alice Perrers, the mistress of King Edward III, infected him with the gonorrhoea from which he was to die. Unrepentant, and greedy to the end as she had been in all their relations, she removed the rings from his fingers as soon as he had died, and kept them for herself.

4 *Embarrassing Relations*

The Earl of Dudley was forced to apologise publicly to Princess Michael of Kent for circulating a scurrilous poem about her. He said that he had only showed it to close friends – including Princess Margaret, who is reported to have fallen off her chair laughing – and had written it to cheer up his wife. The Earl had alleged that Lady Dudley, a '50s film starlet, had suffered extreme embarrassment during a visit to the USA when she accompanied the Princess as unofficial lady-in-waiting. She had had to leave a cinema in order to avoid the spectacle of Princess Michael canoodling in the back row with Elizabeth Taylor's then-husband, US Senator John Warner.

'1985 was a very bad year for me,' said the Princess. The revelation that the father she 'worshipped' was an honorary member of Hitler's SS was followed by the sensational allegation that she was having an affair with a baby-faced Texan billionaire who was once observed queueing for half an hour for a taxi at Victoria station on the way to meet the Princess at an address only two blocks away.

Exhausted by public scrutiny, Prince and Princess Michael accepted the invitation of an Argentinian arms dealer to cruise the Mediterranean on his yacht. Carlos Perdomo, according to a spokesman, 'didn't supply any of the big stuff during the Falklands War – only highly technical back-up equipment'. (Prince Philip's three sisters, all of whom married Germans, were not invited to his wedding in 1947. His sister Sophie was particularly unwelcome, as her husband was an intimate of Goering, the head of the Luftwaffe during the war.)

5 Royal Food

At one of the last garden parties given by Queen Victoria, it was so hot in the royal tea tent that one of the ladies fainted. A quick-thinking Guards officer drew his sword and grandly cut a hole in the tent to let in some air. His weapon pierced the backside of an unfortunate waitress standing without.

Expecting the Shah of Persia for a short visit in 1873, Queen Victoria was surprised by some of the details of his preferences, which were sent on ahead. The list included the following desiderata:

'His Majesty generally dines alone, and prefers to have his meals on the carpet. For that purpose a moveable carpet should be kept ready, whereupon his servants will put the dishes, etc., brought to the door by the English servants. The Shah does not like to cut up his meats.'

His habits indeed turned out to be more unusual than the memorandum had promised. During the Shah's residence, it was observed with disgust that he failed to use the lavatories, preferring to go wherever the spirit moved him. He organised a boxing match in the garden. When he was taken on a tour of a prison and shown the gallows,

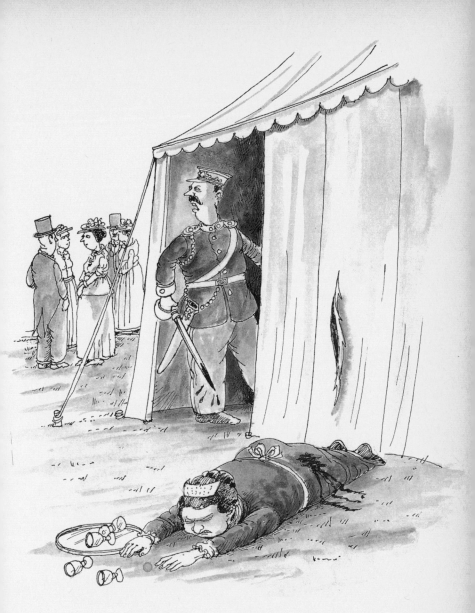

'Fetch a doctor, a lady's fainted in here.'

he asked to see it in use, and when he was told that there were no hangings on the schedule, he directed them to use one of his suite. There was a serious rumour that he had actually had one of his own servants executed with a bow string and had the corpse buried somewhere in the palace gardens.

Buckingham Palace garden staff are said to remain conscious of the possibility of discovering some ancient Mohammedan bones in the herbaceous borders.

Sir Michael Shea, the Queen's press secretary, staying in the same hotel as she in Dar-es-Salaam for the Commonwealth Conference in 1979, discovered a huge rat in his room. When he spoke to the manager about it, wondering amiably how the rat had got all the way up to the sixth floor, the manager, just as amiably replied: 'Oh, no, sir, he is not climbing up the stairs, he is coming down from the top floor where the restaurant is.'

At a large luncheon party in Biarritz attended by King Edward VII, a Portuguese duchess picked up the place

'Inform the Shah that this is not the carpet we've set
aside for his meals.'

... discovered a huge rat in his room.

card of the man next to her and said: 'Kep-pel ... Kep-pel ... How very odd of you to have the same name as the King's mistress.' She was speaking, unsurprisingly, to the King's mistress's husband.

Although they are not notorious masochists, it seems that the Scottish Women's Institute once asked Prince Philip to address their gathering. He began his speech by saying, 'You know, British women can't cook. They are good at decorating food, but they have an inability to cook.'

Possibly this was said in a fit of pique. A short time before, the Queen had put a stop to Prince Philip's fad of cooking the royal family's breakfast sausages every morning in an electric frying pan he kept on the dining room table. She pointed out that Buckingham Palace was still suffused with their less-than-delicate odour at luncheon time.

The Times reported in 1985 that the usually compliant 'Rent-a-Royal' (as Princess Michael of Kent is known for her announcement that 'My husband and I will go anywhere for a hot meal') astonished the assembled cast and VIPs at a celebration for the thousandth episode of the television soap opera *Emmerdale Farm* by complaining, 'I've never seen or heard of this show and I have spent six hours on a train to spend two hours here.'

When she opened a proletarian roadside restaurant the previous year there had been no such complaint, and she was photographed wreathed in merry smiles for the occasion.

Typically of a man who rewarded any sign of human behaviour in his children with terrifying tantrums, King George V indulged his evil-tempered pet parrot, Charlotte, to the most disgusting extent. The hideous grey and pink creature was encouraged to roam the breakfast table, staggering among the plates to pick at a boiled egg here, helping herself to marmalade there. Naturally the feathered fiend in her rapture tended to deposit piles of parrot guano on the tablecloth. The King would simply slide a mustard pot over the evidence.

'I feel hungry, let's go and officially open a restaurant.'

'More mustard pots!'

King George I died of apoplexy in his coach after stuffing himself with melons.

King John is said to have died following a surfeit of peaches and cider at the age of 49, and Henry I from ptomaine poisoning after feasting on too many unfresh eels.

6   *Royal Drama*

In 1955 *Beau Brummell* was chosen as the film to which the monarch would be subjected in the yearly ordeal which was then known as The Royal Command Performance. This particular cinematic extravaganza featured two of the Queen's ancestors. George III was shown as a raving lunatic, and his son, the future George IV, as a snivelling crybaby pleading to be allowed to marry 'the woman he loved'. The Queen was so furious that she complained to the Prime Minister, and asked that the name of the event be changed (lest it be thought that the sovereign had chosen the film) to 'The Royal Variety Performance'.

Robert Morley, who portrayed the mad King George, when told of the Queen's annoyance said: 'It wasn't the most tactful thing to show her.'

There is an echo of this in Queen Victoria's reaction to Thackeray's lectures on the Four Georges. Irritated by his sneering tone, she refused when the time came, to allow him to be buried in Poets Corner.

Queen Mary, who loved going to the theatre, always went backstage after the play. On one such occasion she had seen Gertrude Lawrence in a play by Daphne du Maurier at the Aldwych Theatre. Afterwards, passing down the line of actors backstage, the Queen came to Miss Lawrence, and said how much she had enjoyed herself, except that she had found it quite impossible to hear the ends of the sentences.

'Do you hear?' said Gertrude Lawrence animatedly to the cast, 'Now you've all got to *speak up!*' 'Not all of them,' said Queen Mary firmly. 'Just you.'

On a trip to Hollywood, Prince Andrew, who as a child was rumoured to be mentally deficient, mistook himself for one of the Marx Brothers and sprayed a group of press photographers with paint. This whitewash did not amuse its victims, and one of them sued for damage to his camera. The Queen paid up after giving the Prince a wigging.

'Can you hear me now?'

Captain Mark Phillips, who was voted 'Male Personality Who Did The Most To Promote Hairstyles in 1977' by the Birmingham branch of the National Hairdressers Federation (beating Jeremy Thorpe and Terry Wogan . . .), is the only registered failure of the Television Interview Training Consultancy. It was hoped that they might train him to put himself over well on television so that eventually his nickname 'Fog' might fade away ('He's thick and wet, that's why we call him that.') After trying everything, the consultancy threw in the towel. 'He was bloody hopeless,' said his tutor. 'Eventually I told him just to keep quiet and keep smiling.'

Since the Princesses Elizabeth and Margaret were only allowed to leave the fastness of Windsor Castle during the war for trips to the dentist in London, they were understandably enraged the day in 1943 when what they thought was going to be a special treat turned out to be a poetry reading by Edith Sitwell in aid of the Allies. The turbaned, sibylline poetess bored them into predictable fidgets.

Princess Margaret, behaving oddly after being told by her doctors that her liver would not survive a heavy intake of whisky, surprised friends at a dinner party she attended in Warwickshire by sitting down at the piano and running through her entire repertoire of hymns, ancient and modern. 'For reasons not readily apparent,' one guest reported, 'the Princess started playing hymns and it went on for two hours. No one dared stop her.'

After the death of her husband, King George VI, who knew all there was to know about rhododendrons, the Queen Mother sought consolation through a medium, whom she hoped would be able to put her in contact with her husband on the Other Side. She invited a clairvoyant called Lilian Bayley to Clarence House to conduct a seance. The unconventional experiment was apparently not repeated when the King, wisely, decided not to make an appearance.

7 *Royal Fashion*

In 1981, while stationed at the Culrose Naval Base, Prince Andrew (who was born in a lavatory in Buckingham Palace) attempted to grow a beard. In the allowed three-week period the beard never fully developed, leaving Lieutenant Commander David Warren no alternative but to order the Prince to remove it. On receiving the order, Prince Andrew was said to have sulked all afternoon.

When the Queen was only three (by which time she had mastered the court curtsey) it somehow got out that her nursery, all its trimmings and most of the infant wardrobe, was in yellow. Pink and blue fell out overnight. There was a mania for buttercup and Selfridge's reported that they had sold out of anything in yellow. *Time* magazine put the little princess on their cover for setting a major fashion trend.

A rumour was circulated throughout Lagos by one of the Queen's loyal subjects that the correct etiquette upon meeting royalty includes the removal of one's headgear. Consequently, there was a great rush on the local outfitters as Nigerians in their hundreds and thousands purchased hats for the purpose of removing them. It is for occasions such as these that the Queen has been schooled in the art of keeping a straight face.

Queen Victoria's own distinctive lace bonnet played a part in African hat lore. At his request, the Queen gave a visiting West African chief one of her widow's caps with long white streamers. 'I should like to be the only chief entitled to wear it. I will pass it on to my successors,' he said proudly upon receiving it. One of Queen Victoria's granddaughters used to show a photograph of him in full regalia, with the Queen's lace cap on his head, surmounted by a top hat.

It was about the same period when the American jazz trumpeter Louis Armstrong called Princess Margaret 'One real hip chick' that she demonstrated this in public.

'He'd like you to wear one of his in return, ma'am.'

While on a visit to Africa she acknowledged the leave-taking bow of the Governor of Kenya, Sir Stanley Baring, with the words, 'See you later, alligator.' The correct response to this, as he was later informed, would have been, 'In a while, crocodile.' The governor is said to have been sorry not to have played his part in the exchange.

On her state visit to Paris in 1855, Queen Victoria hoped to charm the fashionable French. In the event her get-up, which would surely have caused quite a stir even in England, was much remarked upon. She arrived carrying a very large handbag on which one of her daughters had embroidered a gaudy parrot, nearly as large. For the state dinner she wore a dress from which substantial bunches of geraniums projected at irregular intervals, and rings on all her fingers, including her thumbs.

At the sight of her, the band struck up *God Save the Queen* arranged as a polka.

On a trip to Australia in 1985 the Princess of Wales (who distinguished herself by giggling most of the time)

appeared at a dance in Melbourne with a priceless diamond and emerald necklace strapped round her forehead in the style of a Red Indian. Fashion experts, announcing that the effect intended was one of 'flapperish frivolity', added that the attempt to achieve this had fallen flat due to her matronly hairstyle. The valuable necklace, which was a wedding present from the Queen, became temporarily dislodged from its intended position by the strenuous exertions attendant upon dancing with the Prince of Wales, for whom she is reported to have invented the nickname 'Fishface'.

Charged with designing the Prince of Wales's investiture, Lord Snowdon opted for a minimalist approach which produced some ludicrous effects. The Earl, acting as the master of ceremonies, appeared in a costume of his own devising: a natty zip-up outfit in hunting green, belted in black corded silk. The Duke of Norfolk pronounced that Snowdon looked 'like a bell-hop at a hotel'.

In 1981, the Princess of Wales (who once won first prize

in the Fur and Feathers Show at Sandringham) was attacked by the fashion editor of *The Times*. Prudence Glynn wrote an article calling the young woman 'a fashion disaster in her own right', complaining that a strapless evening dress worn by the Princess in one of her first public appearances made her look as if she were sitting in a hip-bath.

Miss Glynn was a voice crying in the wilderness. The press in general considered the frock most fetching, as it provided by far the most generous display of royal mammaries seen hitherto. One writer, recalling 'the black silk taffeta ballgown that the Princess was *almost* wearing ...' won approval for the best description of the dress in question.

In Athens for the state reinterment of one of his dead relations, the young Prince Philip (who won a biscuit-eating competition in Paris when he was 7) was wearing his first silk top hat. He displayed great presence of mind when, in his only reported attack of nerves, he was suddenly overcome with nausea. He removed the new hat and vomited into it.

In more recent years he has used this item of formal headgear to conceal a transistor radio so that he can listen to the cricket results in the Queen's Box at Ascot.

When Roy Mason was summoned unexpectedly to Balmoral for a Privy Council meeting, he felt the odd one out and said, while talking to the Queen, 'I see, Ma'am, that all your ministers are in their tweeds.' The Queen smiled and tapped a finger on his chest. 'How useful a string vest is, Mr Mason,' graciously making him feel more comfortable in his lightweight suit and transparent nylon shirt.

Queen Mary, who considered her legs her 'best feature', was rather thrilled when fashion in the 'twenties decreed that skirts should rise considerably above the ankles. Mindful of her husband's conservatism, she decided to use her trusted lady-in-waiting, Lady Airlie, as a guinea-pig to test the King's reactions to the new style. George V, asked by the Queen his opinion of Lady Airlie's new frock, grunted firmly: 'Didn't like it. Too short.' So Queen Mary was forced to abandon the idea of displaying her legs, and continued to wear unfashionable ankle-length skirts until her death in the early 1950s.

Somewhat unfairly a few years later the King ordered Hardy Amies, who had designed bridesmaid dresses for the little Princesses Lilibet and Margaret Rose to wear for the wedding of the Duke of Gloucester, to shorten the dresses: 'I want to see their pretty little knees.'

But the Queen, who had come as a 'beatnik' to a fancy dress party in the '60s, briskly parried Princess Anne's suggestion later in that decade that she should wear a mini skirt with 'I am *not* a film star'.

8 *Money*

Queen Mary's mother, who was rarely out of debt, to put it mildly, was nevertheless very popular, possibly because such things never worried her in the least. She brought the house down when she opened the new Kensington Town Hall, across from Barker's, which was one of her chief creditors. At the end of her speech, Fat Mary, (for that was her usual nickname) declaimed: 'And now I must propose a special vote of thanks to Mr Barker – *to whom we all owe so much*!' Towards the end of her life her debts to tradesmen totalled £70,000.

When he was the Prince of Wales, King George IV was menaced by bailiffs who surrounded the house he was living in with Mrs Fitzherbert, the virtuous woman to whom he was secretly married. They gave him 24 hours to collect the £2000 he owed, which he only managed to do by pawning quantities of jewellery belonging to Mrs Fitzherbert, having long since pawned all of his own valuables. Within a short time his debts were so great that he was obliged to put aside Mrs Fitzherbert, and marry a foreign princess of unparalleled hideosity so that Parliament would vote the money to save him from his baying creditors.

When an anonymous article appeared in *The Times* in 1874, denying that the future King Edward VII was in debt and suggesting that he deserved more money from the civil list, it was strongly rumoured to have been written by the fun-loving heir to the throne himself. A rise in his subsidy was not forthcoming. Several years later, so many newspapers carried scandal about his large debts that the Hotel Bristol, where he was staying in Paris, was besieged with money lenders' agents. The only way the Prefect of Police was able to restore order was to threaten to arrest everyone in the crowd as vagrants. This proved unnecessary, as the Prince of Wales accepted the friendship and its perquisites of several rich tradesmen (simultaneously, it is said, restoring his own credit and ennobling them and descendants.)

9 *Good Sport*

Queen Alexandra, who being Danish was extremely stupid, thought that when playing golf the object of the game was to prevent one's opponent from putting his ball into the hole. This meant that Queen Alexandra staggered about the golf course brandishing her putter and attempting to hit her opponent's ball off the course. Fortunately, being Danish also meant that she was usually quite ineffective.

When George V, Queen Mary and virtually all the Court went to stay with the King of the Belgians in 1922, they were given quarters at opposite ends of the palace, which was a quarter of a mile long and laced with a maze of corridors. Early in their stay a substantial party set out from the King's end in search of the Queen and became hopelessly lost in the labyrinth. Quarrelling bitterly over the best direction in which to proceed were Admiral Lord Beatty, Admiral of the Fleet, and Field Marshal Sir Douglas Haig, who had only a few years before led the biggest army ever to take the field, each abusing the other and assuming command. They were eventually rescued when their shouting prompted the Queen to find the cause of the disagreeable noise.

Once, at a dinner party, Princess Anne talked so exclusively about horses for so long to the man on her left, ignoring the person on her other side, that when he heard her ask for the sugar he placed two lumps in his hand and held them up to her muzzle.

Long before her savage spirit was calmed by a purposeful emulation of Mother Teresa, Princess Anne suffered a kidnapping attempt one evening in the Mall by a man who, it surprised no one to discover, was deranged. He had planned to hold her for a ransom of £3 million. The Princess scarcely turned a hair. 'That man didn't know what he was taking on,' the Queen Mother commented later.

During a performance of the rock musical *Hair* in the 1960s, Princess Anne became so excited by the spectacle that she climbed onto the stage and joined the cast in an orgiastic dance. As she, in her purple trouser suit, was the only person wearing anything at all, she was somewhat conspicuous.

(Shortly after this performance, she was photographed during a visit to a military establishment firing a Sterling sub-machine gun with impressive accuracy. Shooting from the hip, she scored eleven bullseyes.)

At the outbreak of World War II it was decided that Queen Mary should be evacuated to Badminton House, the home of her niece, the Duchess of Beaufort. Arriving with 73 pieces of luggage and 65 servants, the Queen cheerfully applied her formidible energies to country life, a relatively novel experience ('So that's what hay looks like!' she is reported to have said upon seeing some.)

Straightaway she devised the rural pursuit for which she is most celebrated – the 'clearing up' of the Badminton Estate – which caused the Duchess much vexation, as Queen Mary very nearly exterminated all the vegetable life in the vicinity. With the famous toque firmly rivetted to what was politely referred to as her 'transformation' and attended by her 'wooding squad' of equerries, ladies-in-waiting and guests, she was able to indulge her twin passions for tidiness and bossing people about. Only the

Archbishop of Canterbury was a match for her: 'I will *not* go into the woods to pick up twigs!'

But it was the ivy she was after – she hated it, and with her stalwart band cleared 120 acres of the cursed stuff, including a 16-acre fir wood. She ravaged the local villages, stripping all the cottages of the prized ivy which was their sole ornament and ordering the chopping down of any tree which she considered to get in the way of the view.

Relentless in her contribution to the war effort, she motored around the estate on the lookout for any piece of agricultural equipment that some farmer might have been improvident enough to leave lying unattended in a field. These were carted off with great satisfaction by the old Queen under the deluded impression that they were valuable pieces of 'scrap'.

Good relations were eventually restored with the cottagers, and after a six-year stay in the district, Queen Mary was cheered when she joined them in the local pub for a sing-song on VE Day.

10　*Job Satisfaction*

The Queen finally ran out of conversation on a state visit to Norway in 1981. 'How fascinating,' said she, peering up a horse's nostril. Lost for words and possibly experiencing a sense of *déjà vu*, a short time later she observed, 'How fascinating!' as she stared into the 'largest construction hole in the world'.

When she was greeted in Malawi by a horde of fierce warriors dressed in nothing but ankle bells, little furry tails and endearing grins, the Queen ingratiated herself by asking, 'Where *do* they all come from?' She recognised almost all of them as the bankers and businessmen she had met at a reception the previous day.

After the Princess of Wales was given thirty bunches

'When we get to the office we paint ourselves in pin-stripes.'

'I think she's feeling a bit left out.'

of flowers by children after church at Sandringham, the Queen was observed to have been rather neglected. One good little girl initiated 'Queen-Aid' by presenting the empty-handed sovereign with flowers originally intended for the Princess. Her example resulted in a total of six bunches of tulips, daffodils and freesias.

Sir Richard Trehane, the urbane chairman of the Milk Marketing Board, once had the job of showing the Queen round an artificial insemination unit. Half-way into the tour they came to an object which prompted the Queen to ask: 'What is that?' Trehane replied, 'It is a cow's vagina, Ma'am.' The Queen looked up at him without flinching and said, 'Oh well, ask a silly question . . . '

11 *Royal Farts*

King George v's special brand of courtesy prompted him to kick the dog near his heel when a guest at a Sandringham house party farted. The King shouted 'Filthy brute!' at the innocent china dog, which though ugly, was quite odourless, and smashed it to bits.

John Aubrey records in his *Brief Lives* an example of the essential femininity of Elizabeth I. A flatulent courtier disgraced himself in the Queen's presence, for which he was banished to his country estates for seven years. Eventually he was given to understand that he could return to court, which he did, hoping to reintroduce himself quite discreetly. Elizabeth, however, espying him in a corner, welcomed the man heartily, adding 'We have forgot the fart!'

That the Queen actually *prefers* it when things go wrong makes it tempting to agree with those who believe that she herself either invented the following story or circulated it.

It is said that the Queen was sharing a carriage with an African ruler in London on a state visit. During the procession down the Mall one of the horses farted and the Queen said, 'Oh, I'm so sorry.' To which the distinguished visitor replied: 'Do not worry. If you hadn't mentioned it I would have thought it was the horse.'

12   *Religion*

A clergyman staying at Glamis Castle when the Queen spent a summer there as a child, said to her upon leaving that he would send her a book. 'Not about God. I already know everything about Him', said the ten-year-old Princess, in an exchange which would be the first of many illustrating the Queen's omniscience.

In 1936, the Rev. R. A. Jardine, vicar of the small church of St Paul's in Darlington, read in the newspapers that the Duke of Windsor could find no clergyman willing to marry him and Mrs Simpson. Seeing a chance to widen the scope of his ministry, Rev. Jardine wrote to the Duke offering his services, which were accepted. His superiors in the church angrily expressed their disapproval.

The large-nosed, red-faced little cleric later undertook a lecture tour of the United States on the subject of the Duke's wedding, and subsequently opened a Lilliputian chapel in Los Angeles which he called 'Windsor Cathedral'. He distributed business cards to anyone he met, describing himself as Chaplain to the Duke of Windsor.

Edward VII was a somewhat superstitious man, and set great store by his tradition of turning the entire family out of Sandringham House a few minutes before midnight every New Year's Eve. And then on the chiming of midnight, he would lead them into the house and into the New Year. But one year, a young member of the family was late in coming out and the ritual was quite ruined. The King, who ruefully predicted 'We shall have very bad luck this year', was dead the following May.

Preferring his right profile to his left, Edward VIII broke a 300-year-old tradition when he informed the Post Office that he would only allow them to print his 'best' profile. The Crown on the stamps had already been printed, and when the stamps appeared with the King's portrait reversed, *The Times* recorded 'the superstitious anxiety of those who shook apprehensive heads at the new stamps, because the head of King Edward VIII was turned away from the light, and forward into the gloom.'

One of the attractions at the 1924 British Empire Exhibition at Wembley, a statue of the King as Prince of Wales

73

modelled in butter, had the same foreboding aspect. When Bernini's bust of him was completed, King Charles I was sitting in the gardens of Whitehall Palace. The bust was brought to him there, and at the moment that he asked for it to be uncovered so that he could admire the portrait, a hawk flew by with a bird in its beak, a drop of whose blood fell onto the throat of the effigy. The King, who was later beheaded by Cromwell as 'an implacable enemy of the commonwealth of England', is said to have remembered the incident as an omen shortly before his execution.

Towards the end of his life King Henry VII planned a crusade against the Turks. He was forced to abandon the idea when a whip-round at court raised only 11 guineas.

13 *Democracy*

In a gesture which struck his critics as more cringing than egalitarian, King George v received the ministers of the first-ever socialist government wearing a red tie. It was 1924, not six years after his look-alike cousin the Czar had been slaughtered by the Bolsheviks. This was the only time that the British monarch most famous for his sartorial conservatism surprised anybody by his dress, which was an area to which his broad sense of humour was known *not* to apply.

After both the Queen and her first woman Prime Minister wore dresses in the same shade of blue to a banquet, Mrs Thatcher's Private Office enquired of the Palace if there was any way that her staff could check on what the Queen might be wearing on a certain date so that the same duplication would not occur. There came from the Palace an extremely brisk reply which advised Mrs Thatcher not to concern herself, pointing out that, 'The Queen does not notice what other people are wearing.'

Late in life, Queen Mary began to unbend, and during the last war developed the habit of stopping her Daimler to give lifts to soldiers whom she saw walking – whether or not they themselves would have preferred to continue as pedestrians. The Queen was all too often irritated by the American servicemen she picked up, who, not knowing who she was, were insufficiently overwhelmed. So she had little medals struck, with her crown and cipher on, to present to her passengers at the end of the journey – ostensibly as a memento, but actually so that they could express the *correct* degree of gratitude.

In 1948 the Labour Party published a propaganda photograph of an attractive baby, supposedly flourishing under post-war socialism. The features of the child, however, were recognised as belonging to the beautiful infant who grew up to be the Duke of Kent (present job: the promotion of British business interests), who had grown up under pre-war capitalism. The Labour Party apologised for its fraud, and withdrew the pamphlet.

Visiting the sacred Bo tree on a trip to Sri Lanka, the
Queen found that she was expected to remove her shoes
as a gesture of respect. When she did so, the Queen performed an unexpected commercial for Air New Zealand,
whose name and logo were stamped on the navy-blue socks
that a courtier had hastily found for her to wear.

The surge of anti-German hysteria which accompanied
the outbreak of World War I obliged the British royal
family (whose blood was indecently German through and
through) to undergo a rapid de-Teutonification. Whether
George v's family name was 'Wettin' or 'Saxe-Coburg-
Gotha' was uncertain, but a seemly disguise for the family's thoroughly German origins was required. Added to
this, the king's wife, Queen Mary, was a princess of the
House of Teck, and the court pullulated with naturalised
Gleichens, Schleswig-Holsteins and Battenbergs. After a
lot of fussing, George v, his family and descendants
adopted the name of the family seat off the M4 – Windsor.
The Battenbergs translated themselves into Mountbat-
tens; Tecks became Cambridges; and the Schleswig-Hol-

steins obliged by dying out, with the exception of two elderly princesses who suffered the indignity of having to get along as Helena Victoria and Marie Louise – of nothing. The Kaiser was greatly amused by these frantic efforts at camouflage and remarked that he was looking forward to the next performance of *The Merry Wives of Saxe-Coburg-Gotha*.

In an unusual sermon in the cathedral at Christchurch, New Zealand in 1981, the dean, The Very Rev. M. Underhill, reminded the congregation after Prince Philip had read the Lesson that 'other visitors to the cathedral have included Gert and Daisy, those famous entertainers ... Sir Ernest Shackelton, Sir Vivian Fuchs and Ronnie Corbett – all of them read the Lesson, too.'

Overhearing Lord Mountbatten boasting, after Prince Philip had married the Queen, that the name of the royal family was no longer Windsor but Mountbatten, Queen Mary rushed to warn Churchill of his impertinent presumption. Churchill at once summoned the cabinet, and

'That was unfortunate, Prime Minister, your wearing
the same clothes as Her Majesty.'

they advised the Queen to put Mountbatten in his place. A statement was issued, 'That the Queen and her children shall be known as the House and Family of Windsor, and her descendants . . . shall bear the name Windsor.'

In 1969, after the thwarted Mountbatten is said to have encouraged Prince Philip to sulk for eight years, the Queen issued a second declaration, 'after further consideration, replacing the name of Windsor with that of Mountbatten-Windsor . . . to be borne by those descendants of the Queen for whom a surname will be necessary.'

Although stated thus, the change will not take effect until the Queen has great-grandchildren in the male line, (since princes and princesses do not traditionally use a surname). The male grandchildren of Prince Edward and Prince Andrew will sign their cheques as Mountbatten-Windsor. When Princess Anne, who needs no surname, signed the register upon her marriage 'Mountbatten-Windsor', it was thought to be a gesture to her father.

Lord Mountbatten once boasted that the issue of the name, which was his pet project, was the reason for the long gap between the births of Princess Anne and Prince Andrew. Prince Charles used no surname when he signed the register at his wedding.

Twice during the 'phoney war' in 1939, King George VI, mistaking Hitler for a gentleman, drafted letters to the German leader 'as one ex-serviceman to another' in an

'They only had wind-socks.'

attempt to avert war. Neville Chamberlain had to refuse him this gesture each time.

14 *Royal Ceremonial*

A village chief in Botswana, hearing that the Queen was coming on a visit, said confidently, 'Oh yes, Queen Victoria.' 'Oh, no,' he was informed by a member of the Palace reconnaissance party. 'I am afraid that *she* is dead.' 'Well, then,' the chief said huffily, 'Why weren't we invited to the funeral?'

At the coronation of Henry IV, one of the King's shoes dropped off in the procession, and on the way out of the Abbey he lost a spur from the other leg. During the coronation banquet a gust of wind carried the crown from his head, which is reported to have inspired a sense of insecurity in his supporters.

His reign had a few ups and downs and not even after death was he free from nemesis. His corpse was being taken from London by boat for burial at Canterbury Cathedral when a great storm arose. The superstitious sailors threw his body overboard, and substituted another body in the King's coffin. When the coffin was opened in 1823 this story, which for several hundred years had been thought apocryphal, was proved. They found that the royal coffin contained an inner coffin of mean design and quite another shape: the body was dressed in no regalia, but common clothing, and it was surmounted by a cross of twigs.

Possibly unnerved by the spectre of the uncrowned Edward VIII, the operatives at the Coronation of his brother, King George VI, combined to produce a catalogue of relative disasters which the new king furiously recorded in his diary. The Archbishop's thumb covered the words of the oath; the Lord Chamberlain's hands shook so much that the King had to fix the belt of the sword of state himself; the place in the Bible was lost more than once. A chaplain fainted; the crown was put on the King's head the wrong way round; and after he was finally crowned, the slowly-pacing King was brought to an abrupt halt by one of the bishops standing on his robe. 'I had to tell him to get off it pretty sharply as I nearly fell down,' noted the King.

The present Queen's coronation went off seamlessly, with a twentieth-century theatrical verisimilitude added by the seven coaches which had been sold by the Royal Mews to Alexander Korda being borrowed back to complete the impression of splendour.

But most previous coronations have had an over-sufficiency of those fruity incidents which made history three-dimensional.

'Come on one of you, it's a great honour being a
substitute royal corpse.'

The coronation of George III was delayed for two days when the workmen went on strike, and then on the morning of the great day, the canopy, the chair of state and the sword of state were nowhere to be found. During the service, the Bishop of Salisbury got so muddled that he referred in his sermon to the extraordinary number of years the King had already sat on the throne. Since he could barely be heard through the din of what one witness described as 'the general clattering of forks, knives, plates and glasses' that the congregation wielded as they munched their way informally through the six-hour service, few noticed.

At the official coronation banquet afterwards, the King's hereditary champion rode in, gorgeously attired, to throw down the gauntlet, a symbolic challenge to the King's enemies. His steed, which had been hired for the occasion from Astley's Circus, offered a rather old-fashioned challenge, by presenting its rump to the King.

King George III was the last monarch to style himself King of France, which was such a fantastic conceit that no one remarked upon the oddity of two actors being brought in to impersonate the Dukes of Normandy and Aquitaine 'come to give Fealty'. The Lord High Steward made matters worse by saying, 'I have taken care that the *next* coronation shall be regulated in the best manner possible.'

The next coronation, that of George IV, was distinguished by the employment of prize fighters as the King's pages, the wisdom of which became obvious when his famously indiscreet estranged wife, Caroline, with whom the King had not spoken in years, attempted to force herself into the ceremony by banging her fists on the doors of the Abbey, and signalling her frustration at not being crowned queen by a high-pitched wailing.

Queen Victoria's coronation might easily have been invalid. The Bishop of Bath and Wells turned over two pages at once at the end of the service, thereby omitting a part of it, and advised the Queen that she might retire, the coronation having ended. The Queen trooped off in her regalia and found the sub-dean in a state of agitation, insisting that she return and complete the ritual. So the Queen trooped back again, into the debris of the Abbey, where bottles of wine and half-eaten sandwiches littered the aisles, and repeated the formula from the missing bits on.

By this time, she was in rather a temper, since the

'Never mind the ring, see if you can get the crown off!'

coronation ring, having been specially altered for her little finger, had been ceremonially jammed onto a larger one by mistake, where it had got quite stuck and throbbed painfully. She was unable to remove it, and had to go to bed with it on.

Edward VII's crowning had to be postponed when he came down with appendicitis. On the second try, not *too* much went wrong on the altar. The Archbishop of Canterbury fell over and had to be caught by three bishops conveniently kneeling nearby, and fun-loving Queen Alexandra didn't complain when the holy oil was dripped down her nose. The best part was off-stage. The Marchioness of Londonderry lost her coronet down the peeresses' lavatory, from which it was fetched out by a doctor with a pair of forceps. As this happened in the middle of the ceremony, it caused some speculation.

At the great Exhibition in 1851, as Handel's *Halleluja Chorus* was being performed, a Chinaman with perfect composure, seeming to expect a good reception, made a bow to the Queen. The officials, assuming that he was a last-minute representative of the Emperor of China, placed him conspicuously in the stately procession of ambassadors.

It was later found that the imposing figure in a blue satin robe was a sea captain called Hee Sing who had brought his junk into the Thames in the hopes of exhibiting it to the throng that had crowded into the capital for the Great Exhibition. The Chinaman made a lot of money through the attendant publicity.

15 *Drink*

After a party in Kensington Palace that she had given for a small number of friends, including the ballet dancer Rudolph Nureyev, Princess Margaret was given the tragic news that four bottles of a sort of vodka that is rare in this country had vanished. The next morning the crafty Princess, after telephoning every guest, unmasked the culprit by a process of elimination.

It was commonly assumed because of his blotchy red complexion and insensate rages that King George v, whose greatest interests were the weather, shooting, and his stamp collection, was actually a hopeless dipsomaniac. The Austrian ambassador reported that at pious meetings in the East End of London prayers were said for Queen Mary and the royal children, 'begging the protection of the Lord on their unhappy, drunkard's home'.

Queen Anne, who enjoyed a passionate friendship with Sarah, Duchess of Marlborough, was so fat that she had to be carried throughout her coronation in a large chair. When she died (of drink, it was generally assumed, due to her extreme fondness for brandy) the coffin had to be made as wide as it was long. Her consort, Prince George of Denmark, was notoriously inept and stupid, and boring in the extreme. He confined his interests to drinking and making ships in bottles.

Queen Victoria wasn't nearly as Victorian as Albert 'the Good'. She was so enthusiastic about what she thought were authentic Highland customs that there were always two barrels of good malt whisky available to the servants Downstairs. Her coachman kept a bottle handy under the seat. Fresh bottles of the life-giving fluid were given to each guest before setting out to hunt the stag, and drinks were poured out unwatered before breakfast. At dusk, the stalkers swallowed whatever was left, and stumbled back from the hills as drunk as the guests.

At a famous ball half the tenants and staff ended up

insensible on the floor but the Queen understood that it was part of Highland life. She herself preferred to drink claret, 'strengthened' as she put it, with malt whisky.

When her faithful retainer, John Brown, who horrified the rest of the family by often being several sheets to the wind, fell over while out walking with the Queen, she defended him by saying, 'I distinctly felt a slight earthquake shock myself.' Until the day she died (according to her doctors from eating too much ice cream and strawberries), she had a 'nightcap' in bed.

During a drinks party two weeks after the death of George v, for whom everyone was wearing mourning, the future Duchess of Windsor told the notorious gossip Chips Channon that she hadn't worn black stockings since she gave up doing the can-can.

After delivering a speech on road safety to a luncheon meeting in 1957, Prince Philip drove his Lagonda into a car which emerged from a side street, interposing itself between the Prince and his chosen route.

16 *Royal and Rude*

Mrs Thatcher, newly Prime Minister, and enjoying it, made her first mistake at a Buckingham Palace garden party. Seeing people waving, she thought the adulation was for her and waved back, enthusiastically. The Queen, finally irritated by this, gave her a frosty look and went into the Palace trailed by the corgis.

King George V's sister was accustomed to telephone him every day for a gossip, and once hooted down the line as usual, 'Is that you, you old fool?' The Buckingham Palace operator carefully replied: 'No, Your Royal Highness, His Majesty is not yet on the line.'

Staying at Balmoral for the first time since his marriage to the Queen had lifted him from poverty to grandeur, the

Duke of Edinburgh (who had £8 in the bank on their wedding day) came down to dinner in a borrowed kilt. Embarrassed because it was too short, he made his new father-in-law a deep curtsey and simpered, 'Don't I look beautiful?' The King roared his opinion in blunt Anglo-Saxon.

Irritated by someone at a Small Businessman's Association luncheon, Prince Philip answered the man who had said that no one could make a fortune in Britain any more by saying: 'What about Tom Jones? He's made a million – and he's a bloody awful singer.' The middle-aged Welsh sex-symbol had sung before the Prince in a Royal Variety Show the previous night.

The Prince was obviously in a dissatisfied mood that year, which was 1969, as he also said to a French politician, 'Isn't it a pity that Louis XVI was sent to the guillotine?' And he remarked to the dictator of Paraguay, General Stroessner, that it was 'a pleasant change to be in a country that isn't ruled by its people'. Quick as a flash the Palace Press Office announced that Prince Philip was only referring to 'minor nuisances' like the Lord's Day Observance Society.

Six years before, the Prince had said of his public image: 'I know I'm rude, but it's fun'.

'We're very honoured to have you come here and insult us.'

Princess Michael of Kent, of whom the Queen once said, 'She is far too grand for us', was infuriated when she and her husband were given a suite of rooms that she considered too small during their first Christmas at Windsor Castle.

At a state banquet in Brazil in 1968, Prince Philip got some of his own medicine from a general of that nation, who was all decked out in medals but minus the dark glasses. The Prince, who was wearing a chestful of medals himself, asked the general where he had got his. The general replied that he had got them in the war. 'The war?,' countered Prince Philip. 'I didn't think Brazil was in the war that long.' 'At least, sir,' shot back the general, 'I didn't get them for marrying my wife.'

Queen Alexandra used to say when reminded of the King's fury whenever she was late, 'That's all right – keep him waiting, it will do him good!' Her very Danish sense of humour obliged the King in consequence always to have a mistress in order to have any civilised conversation at all.

The Queen Mother gave a rare demonstration of ambi-dexterity during the royal visit to South Africa in 1947. Without alteration to her customary benevolent smile, she simultaneously protected her family from the attentions of a giant Zulu by beating him off with the parasol in her left hand, while serenely acknowledging the cheering crowd with her right hand in that familiar circular gesture.

Eventually she understood that the man who had charged through the police cordon to attach himself to her car was clutching a 10-shilling note, which he wished to offer to Princess Elizabeth on her 21st birthday.

'It was the worst mistake of my life,' the Queen Mother commented later.

On a trip to Canada, having just descended from his aeroplane, Prince Philip was asked politely by the chairman of the reception committee:

'How was your flight?'

'Have you ever flown in a plane?' asked Prince Philip in reply.

'Yes, Your Royal Highness, often.'

'Well, it was just like that,' the Prince humourlessly concluded.

In spite of the decline in her fortunes occasioned by her ceasing to be King Edward VII's mistress, the celebrated beauty Lilly Langtry kept her good opinion of herself. At a charity fête, she was dispensing cups of tea. They cost five shillings, but if Lilly took the first sip, the charge went up to a guinea. The King, after a stately perambulation, reached Lilly's place. Unasked, she poured out some tea and touched her lips to the rim of the teacup before handing it to him. The King set the tea down with the brusque order: 'I should like a clean one, please.' His former mistress served him in silence. He put two gold sovereigns in the dish and strode off.

Making a speech in Ottawa once, Prince Philip (whom Clive Jenkins has called the 'best argument for republicanism since George III') gave a classic illustration of the abrasiveness for which he has become famous, when he said: 'The monarchy exists not for its own benefit, but for that of the country. We don't come here for our health. We can think of better ways to enjoy ourselves.' A few weeks later the Queen's portrait was removed from the new Canadian banknotes and replaced with pictures of past Canadian premiers.

Gaily chatting with the Queen at a party for Sir Robert Mayer, the geriatric beauty Lady Diana Cooper suddenly realised who it was she was talking to, and recalled that she had neglected to curtsey. 'Oh, I am so sorry,' she said, 'I didn't recognise you without your crown.'

A faintly similar attack of party nerves was visited upon the celebrated author E.M. Forster, who in his dotage attended the wedding of Lord Harewood at St James's Palace. He was asked if he would like to be presented to the Queen Mother by a friend, who gesticulated in her direction. 'Oh, dear, I thought that was the wedding cake', sighed Forster.

Most unlucky of all was the elderly gentleman who found himself in conversation with Princess Mary, George VI's sister, without being able to recall exactly who she was. 'And tell me,' he cosily asked, 'What's your brother doing these days?' 'He's still King,' she replied.

17 Foreign Affairs

Inspecting the presents which had flooded in to the palace for the Queen's wedding, her grandmother, no fan of Indian independence, was deeply disgusted by Gandhi's gift, a piece of his own weaving, which she suspected of being a loin-cloth. 'What a horrible thing!' she tutted, sweeping past it. On a subsequent viewing, Princess Margaret prudently hid the offending article from view behind specimens of the thousands of nylon stockings that the Queen had been sent by American female admirers.

It is not certain what Queen Mary would have made of the gold chain-mail pinafore which an Arab ruler presented to the Queen on her 1979 tour of the Gulf.

Attending the inevitable agricultural show in New Zealand, the Queen and Prince Philip made an unwitting detour off the official red carpet and went down another laid at an angle to it by an enterprising exhibitor. The royal couple sauntered amiably down the 40 yards of maverick carpet and ended up inspecting a two-room holiday chalet which had not been listed in their schedule.

The Queen, who is sometimes amused when things go wrong, was nevertheless surprised to find no reception committee to greet her when she landed in Dubrovnik on a visit in 1973. They had all rushed off before she arrived, after being mistakenly informed that the Queen's flight had been diverted to Titograd. It is not recorded whether the disappearing reception committee was allowed to reassemble for the greeting ceremony.

The commercial refrigeration plant deemed necessary to achieve an acceptably Northern European temperature for the Queen during one of her many visits to Africa was so effective that the room had to be defrosted before the Queen could make herself at home.

The British royal family have always seemed to regard travelling as an occupational hazard, and are often unimpressed by the world's best-loved tourist attractions. King George V, whose most famous quote is 'Bugger Bognor!' was fiercely xenophobic. 'Abroad is awful. I know. I have been,' said the home-loving monarch. He particularly hated Naples, saying that the harbour was full of dead dogs. His wife, Queen Mary, reported from Egypt: 'The Sphinx I thought particularly disappointing.' Her father-in-law, King Edward VII, went to Rome and announced: 'You look at two or three mouldering stones and are told it's the Temple of Something.'

Continuing the family tradition, Prince Charles replied when he was asked if he had been touched by the beauty of the Taj Mahal, 'Well, I did bang my head against the ceiling at one point.' The Queen, less anxious to please, announced when she was shown Niagara Falls: 'It looks very damp.'

The Windsors have ever felt exempt from the need to affect the conventional pieties when it comes to art with a capital A. At an exhibition, George V took one look at a painting by Cézanne and hailed Queen Mary: 'Come over here May, there's something that will make you laugh!'

The Queen could be forgiven for agreeing with President Jefferson that Britain and the United States are separated by a common language. When Nixon's ambassador to Britain, Walter Annenberg, was presented to the Queen she asked how he was settling into his new home. 'Very well, Ma'am,' came the reply, 'except for some discomfiture owing to elements of refurbishment.'

Ostensibly to secure an important steel contract, the Queen consented to visit Morocco in 1980 at the invitation of King Hassan. Although she had been warned by Princess Margaret that 'going to Morocco is more like being kidnapped', she was unprepared for what awaited her.

Instead of attending the welcoming lunch that had been scheduled, King Hassan decided to play golf. Then he evicted the Queen's two most senior ladies-in-waiting from the guest palace. In the evening he was an hour and a half late for the state banquet, which included two electrical black-outs and an unscheduled civic reception, with dignitaries looking identical in fezzes.

Next day the Queen thought she *was* being kidnapped

when, en route with the king for a picnic lunch, she was loaded into that irascible monarch's limousine and driven along rough dusty roads at a terrifying speed. Seven times during this ordeal the car stopped abruptly, and she was bundled into a different car before they reached the foot of the Atlas Mountains, where a tent had been prepared. The king then disappeared into an air-conditioned caravan, leaving the Queen sitting hot, hungry and maddened in the crowded tent. After an hour of this she indicated that she wanted to leave but none of the Moroccan chauffeurs would agree to drive her away. By four o'clock, no food had arrived, but the king appeared, saying he had been busy making sure that everything was perfect.

The Queen led the cheering when her plane finally left Moroccan soil.

18   *Edward VIII*

At the time of Edward VIII's Abdication, the socialist politician and trade union leader J.H. Thomas complained to Harold Nicolson: 'And now 'ere we 'ave this obstinate little man with 'is Mrs Simpson. Hit won't do, 'Arold, I tell you that straight. I know the people of this country. I *know* them.'

When the German army invaded Paris, the Duke and Duchess of Windsor fled to Portugal. The British government, in receipt of intelligence that Hitler intended to capture the Duke and his wife and restore them to the throne in the event of a German victory, sent three flying boats to bring them back to London. The Duke refused to return, obliging Churchill to threaten him with court martial (he had never resigned as a serving member of the army). A compromise was reached when the Duke agreed to go straight to the Bahamas (which the Duchess referred to as 'Elba') to serve as governor. Until shortly before the end of the war, the Duke was still in touch with the Germans on the subject of his potential utility in the event of their victory over the British. He resigned from his post two weeks before Hitler shot himself.

Unable to reconcile herself to the fact that by marrying her, the ex-King had ceased to be an important world figure, the Duchess of Windsor engineered a 'state visit' to Germany, ostensibly to study housing and working conditions.

The British Ambassador was ordered to refuse to see them. They were left entirely in the hands of a maniacal Nazi who later hanged himself rather than face the Nuremburg trials. For two weeks the Duke and Duchess were greeted everywhere they went (in a black Mercedes-Benz with ear-piercing siren and a radio blaring out German martial music) with the Nazi salute and 'Heil Windsor!' The Duke of Windsor responded with the Nazi salute and 'Heil Hitler!' They stayed with Hitler and afterwards he said of the Duke: 'His abdication was a severe loss to us ... the Duchess would have made a good Queen.'

After this, the Duke and Duchess, in the face of an uproar of furious criticism, confined their lime-light grabbing efforts to an appeal for 'world peace' broadcast on the American NBC radio network just as the new King and Queen were about to undertake an official state visit to the United States.

The Duke of Windsor, who used to lace the cocktails at his parties with Benzedrine 'to make the party go' was congratulated by Lady Astor on his modern method of kingship, saying that it would make things easier for his successor. She seems to have been one of the few to hold this opinion. During his father's funeral procession, as the coffin was carried into Palace Yard, the royal crown, which was carried on top, shed its jewelled Maltese Cross, which rolled into a gutter. The new King Edward VIII, who was shortly to abdicate, was heard to mutter: 'Christ! What's going to happen next!' A member of Parliament standing nearby commented: 'A fitting motto for the coming reign.'

In 1954, the Duchess of Windsor arrived in England with 35 pieces of luggage. Her secretary explained that the Duchess had brought 'just an ordinary wardrobe for a week's stay'. She was, nevertheless, travelling lighter than on a previous visit, when she had brought all of her jewels – and was relieved of them in a most mysterious way.

She and the Duke of Windsor had come to stay with the Earl and Countess of Dudley in the summer of 1946. It was their first visit to England after the Abdication, and the Duchess, understandably deciding to queen it a bit, had packed the entire arsenal of gems for which she had become so famous. Among them were a great many uncut emeralds which had belonged to Queen Alexandra. The vast trunk containing this treasure ought to have been put in the strong room, but the Duchess grandly ordered that they be kept, according to her custom, under her own maid's bed. They never got there. As they nestled snobbishly together in the trunk, waiting for footmen to move them, the gems were snatched by thieves who were not observed by the detective guarding the house and had not attracted the attention of the dogs.

It was odd that the jewels were never seen or heard of again. Queen Mary herself was suspected, so enraged was she known to be that her son had adorned the hated Mrs Simpson with royal jewels. The Duchess of Windsor never wavered from her conviction that they had been taken by the Secret Service on the express orders of the royal family.

The Duchess's comments afterwards ensured that whatever sympathy she might have had for her loss was restricted to the more fortunate classes. When asked by a reporter what jewellery she had been wearing on the night of the robbery she snapped: 'Anyone but a fool would know that with tweeds or any daytime clothes one wears gold, and with evening clothes one wears platinum.'

19   *Endurance*

Christopher Sykes, the royal sycophant *sine qua non* squandered his fortune on King Edward VII, and was so unfailingly deferential that the then Prince of Wales used to pour brandy over his head, and amuse himself by stubbing cigars out on the courtier's hand to see, as he put it, whether smoke would emerge from the man's ears unimpeded by whatever his brain might constitute. Once he put a dead seagull in Sykes's bed; which was as nothing compared to the time he dressed the poor fellow in a full suit of armour and sent him out, drunk, into the Mall. Eventually Sykes, possibly hoping it would put an end to these games, went bankrupt, but his royal patron loyally organised for his richer friends to put up enough money to keep Sykes out of jail.

The Queen's father, George VI, who had a framed notice reading 'Cleanliness is next to Godliness' in his bathroom in Buckingham Palace, was an extremely shy man. One consequence of this was that he found it difficult to end a conversation – a handicap which exhausted his visitors, since etiquette required that no one could dismiss himself, or leave before the King. George Bernard Shaw, no longer

'You can't arrest me, I'm drunk by royal appointment.'

able to endure a flagging interview, speeded up the inevitable by ostentatiously fishing about for his pocket watch, and then giving it a long, cool look.

Despite going for three days without food, drink or the consolation of any of his wives in an attempt to ensure fine weather for the Queen's visit in 1977, the chief of the Waimaro tribe greeted the sovereign in a torrential downpour with tiny green frogs trying to leap up his grass skirt.

Seated next to a deaf bishop at a luncheon party in the country, Queen Mary, finding that she had a piece of gristle in her fodder, considerately bethought herself of the dogs who were also in attendance, and who, since it was wartime, were also on short rations. 'Here,' she said to the deaf bishop, 'Give this to the little chap' – handing him the gristle. The modest clergyman, thinking it was a royal command, popped it into his mouth, disappointing the little dog. He chewed valiantly, and eventually managed to dispatch the morsel.

'I've already given you one bit!'

20   *Royal Children*

Prince Albert's father was so notoriously licentious that, according to the distinguished biographer Giles St Aubyn, 'there were few deviations from morality or convention he had not pioneered'. Aware also that his wife's family harboured some notable eccentrics (including her Uncle Ernest, who was reputed to have murdered his valet), the Prince Consort thought it wise to rule his children with a rod of iron, lest any disagreeable family traits emerge.

The future Edward VII, as heir to the throne, was forbidden 'self-indulgent lounging, hands in the pockets, slouching gait,' etc. etc. In addition to the usual tortures that children undergo in the schoolroom, the young Edward was subjected to military exercises under a drill sergeant; was forced to learn bricklaying and housework; and submitted to periodic examinations by a phrenologist who assessed the bumps in his skull for moral and intellectual progress. He was entirely isolated from other boys. By the time he was 12 his tutor reported that the child 'had a great pleasure in giving pain to others'.

Surprisingly, the Prince survived this treatment, and turned into a warm-hearted soul who once received a silver inkwell to acknowledge his kindness in leading a blind man across the road – an act which he hoped had been unobserved.

Queen Mary, who in her latter years did not crave anonymity, was out driving during the last war when her car passed a school near Bath. The uniformed schoolgirls, liberated for the day, constituted a crowd as far as Queen Mary was concerned. The unmistakably regal figure (sitting according to custom in an elevated seat to be more visible) was unpleasantly surprised when the girls merely stared in 'a desultory, adenoidal kind of way'. To give them a cue, the old Queen waved and smiled, but still they did not respond. '*Cheer*, little idiots, can't you!' exclaimed the Queen testily.

When 'Crawfie', governess to the Princesses Elizabeth and Margaret, married a man who worked in a bank the young couple were treated royally. They were given a grace-and-favour apartment in Kensington Palace; the former governess received a pension, and Queen Mary decorated the flat with Victorian furniture and flower prints. The King appointed her a Commander of the Royal Victorian Order.

The former Miss Crawford is reputed to have thought these rewards for her service inadequate, hoping to be made a Dame of the Order, and a lady-in-waiting to her former charge.

After three years of enjoying these perquisites, she was the first to 'do a Crawfie' – the phrase that has been used by the royal family ever since to suggest disloyalty. She burst into print with *The Little Princesses*, a memoir which her benefactors found very disagreeable. The future Queen, it was thought, was portrayed as a prig; little Princess Margaret as an arrogant tyrant; and the King and Queen as lacking interest in their children. They were furious that trusty Miss Crawford allowed their privacy to be invaded for personal gain.

Her career as a tatler was abruptly ended when she reported both Royal Ascot and the Trooping of the Colour all in a gush for *Woman's Own* – in a year they were both cancelled due to a rail strike.

21 *Royal Deaths*

Charles I, executed on the orders of Cromwell, was given an expert stroke which sliced clean through the fourth vertebra of the royal neck. In 1813, the royal surgeon, coveting this relic, purloined it after a post-post-post-mortem, and employed the souvenir as a salt cellar for the next 30 years. He was obliged to surrender it when Queen Victoria found out about his unusual table decoration, and ordered its return.

The body of King Henry v's wife, Catherine de Valois, was dug up during a 'refurb' of Westminster Abbey during the reign of Henry VIII. The mummified corpse was put on show, and remained accessible to casual visitors until 1776. On his thirty-sixth birthday, Samuel Pepys paid the verger a shilling and recorded, 'I had the upper part of her body in my hands, and I did kiss her mouth, reflecting that I did first kiss a Queen.'

The tomb in which the corpse of Richard I lay in Westminster Abbey had a opening through which the skull might be touched. In 1776, a schoolboy removed the King's jaw-bone, which passed down through the family until a right-thinking descendant of the boy returned the gruesome heirloom to the Abbey in 1906.

For the 45 years of her reign, Elizabeth I chose never to remove her coronation ring, which eventually grew deeply embedded in her flesh. In her last illness, the doctors, thinking to improve her condition, had it cut away. Within a week the Queen was dead, of an infection in her tonsils. Some at court insisted that it was the symbolic stripping of her queenship that hastened mortality.

After five chops, the executioners finally separated his head from the Duke of Monmouth's body. Belatedly it was realised that, as the illegitimate first-born son of Charles II, it was important that his portrait be painted. The Duke's head was duly sewn back onto the body, the joins painted over, the body dressed and a likeness taken. It now hangs in the National Portrait Gallery.

Although Shakespeare's play of the same name has King Richard II die after being pole-axed by Sir Piers Exton, the king's exhumed body showed no signs of skull fracture. He was actually one of the most famous victims of anorexia nervosa, brought on by depression, dying at the age of 36.

Despite his estranged wife's murderous fancies (Caroline of Brunswick habitually made little wax effigies with horns on them, pierced them with pins and threw them into the fire), King George IV actually died of cirrhosis of the liver. Later generations have realised that this is a common cause of death, affected long-distance by dissatisfied wives. Particularly Danish ones.

Another spurned woman caused the cruel death of Edward
II. His wife, enraged by the King's flagrant homosexual
attachment to the notorious wag Piers Gaveston, arranged
to have a red-hot spit thrust into Edward's bowels through
a horn thrust into his rectum. Less dreamy than Caroline
of Brunswick, and consequently more effective, she was
still obviously possessed of a creative streak.